D1710418

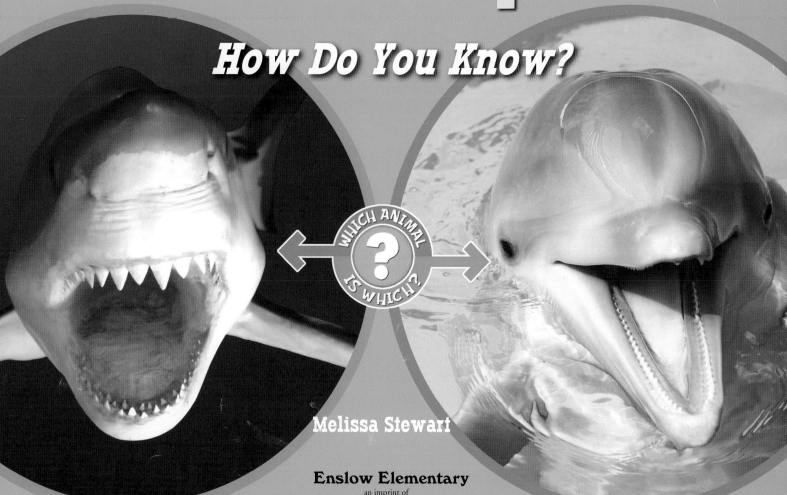

Shark or Dolphin?

How Do You Know?

WHICH ANIMAL ? IS WHICH?

Melissa Stewart

Enslow Elementary
an imprint of
Enslow Publishers, Inc.
40 Industrial Road
Box 398
Berkeley Heights, NJ 07922
USA
http://www.enslow.com

SAYVILLE LIBRARY

Contents

Words to Know

fish (FISH)—An animal that has a backbone and gills. Its body temperature matches the water it is swimming in.

mammal (MAH muhl)—An animal that has a backbone and lungs. It always has the same body temperature. The mother feeds its baby milk.

oxygen (AHK suh jen)—A gas that has no color or smell. Living things need oxygen to live.

predator (PREH duh tur)—An animal that hunts and kills other animals for food.

prey (PRAY)—An animal that is hunted by a predator.

Do You Know?

Which of
these animals
is a shark?
Which one is
a dolphin?
Do you know?

Fish or Mammal?

Sharks

Spotted eagle ray

A shark is a fish. All fish live in the water. A fish has a backbone and gills. Its body temperature changes to match the water it is swimming in.

Butterfly fish

Lionfish

Dolphin

Kangaroo

A dolphin is a **mammal.** Most mammals live on land. A mammal has a backbone and lungs. It always has the same body temperature. The mother feeds its baby milk.

Giraffe

Tamarin

7

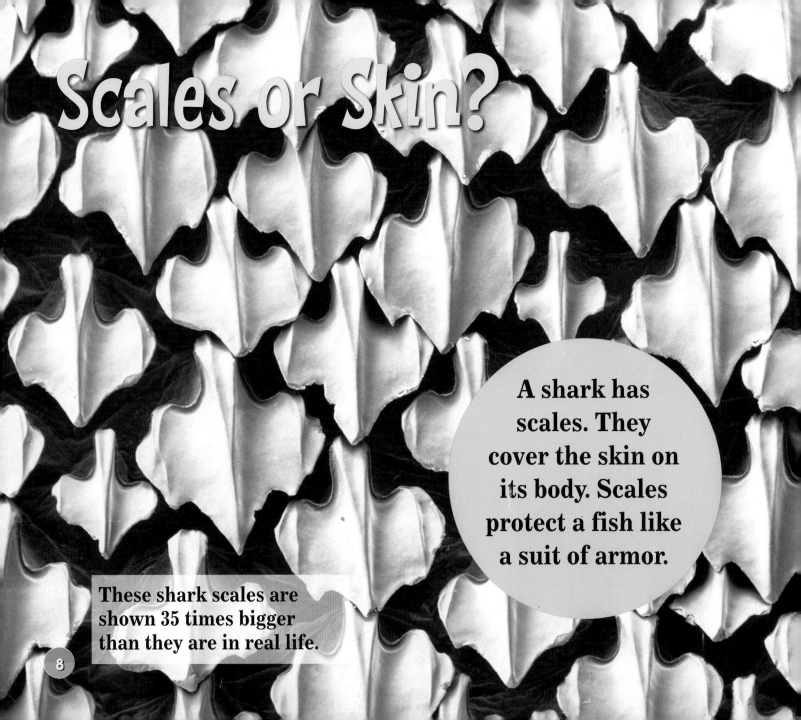

Scales or Skin?

A shark has scales. They cover the skin on its body. Scales protect a fish like a suit of armor.

These shark scales are shown 35 times bigger than they are in real life.

A dolphin does not have scales. A thick layer of fat below the skin keeps a dolphin warm.

Bottlenose dolphin

Tail or Fluke?

A shark has a powerful tail that pushes it through the water. The tail bends from side to side.

Reef shark

Bottlenose dolphins

fluke

A dolphin's
strong fluke
moves up and
down as
it swims.

Gills or Lungs?

A shark has **gills**. Gills take oxygen from the water. Sharks need oxygen to live and grow.

A dolphin has lungs.
Lungs take oxygen
from the air.
A dolphin breathes
through a hole
on the top of
its head.

13

Pup or Calf?

Tiger shark pup

A young shark is called a pup. Mother sharks do not take care of their pups.

14

Atlantic bottlenose
dolphins

A baby dolphin is
called a calf.
It drinks milk from
its mother's body.
The calf stays with
its mother for three
to six years.

Smell or Sound?

A shark uses smell to find food. Some sharks can smell ten thousand times better than you.

Bull shark

A dolphin uses sound to find food. As a dolphin swims, it makes clicking noises. If the sounds hit a fish, the noise bounces back. Then the dolphin grabs its prey.

Atlantic spotted dolphin

Now Do You Know?

This animal is a fish.

Its baby is called a pup.

Scales cover its skin.

Great white shark

It has a powerful tail.

It breathes with gills.

It finds food by smelling.

It's a shark!

This animal is a mammal.

It does not have scales.

Its baby is called a calf.

It has a strong fluke.

Bottlenose dolphin

It breathes with lungs.

It uses sounds to catch prey.

It's a dolphin!

What a Surprise!

Whale shark

A whale shark is longer than two school buses, but it eats tiny ocean creatures.

A killer whale
is not really a whale.
It is the biggest
dolphin in the world.
It eats sea turtles,
penguins, seals, and
sharks. It even eats
other dolphins.

Killer whales

21

Learn More

Books

Nicklin, Flip and Linda. Face to Face with Dolphins. Washington, D.C.: National Geographic, 2007.

Sabuda, Robert and Matthew Reinhart. Encyclopedia Prehistorica: Sharks and Other Sea Monsters. Cambridge, Mass.: Candlewick, 2006.

Schreiber, Anne. Sharks! Washington, D.C.: National Geographic, 2008.

Simon, Seymour. Oceans. New York: HarperCollins, 2008.

Web Sites

Bottlenose Dolphins
http://kids.nationalgeographic.com/Animals/
CreatureFeature/Bottlenose-dolphin

Ocean Adventures, Fun and Games
http://www.pbs.org/kqed/oceanadventures/
funandgames

Shark Tales
http://magma.nationalgeographic.com/
ngexplorer/0505/articles/mainarticle.html

Index

Enslow Elementary, an imprint of Enslow Publishers, Inc.

Enslow Elementary® is a registered trademark of Enslow Publishers, Inc.

Copyright © 2011 by Melissa Stewart

All rights reserved.

No part of this book may be reproduced by any means without the written permission of the publisher.

Library of Congress Cataloging-in-Publication Data

Stewart, Melissa.
  Shark or dolphin? : how do you know? / Melissa Stewart.
    p. cm. — (Which animal is which?)
  Includes bibliographical references and index.
  Summary: "Explains to young readers how to tell the difference between sharks and
    dolphins"—Provided by publisher.
  ISBN 978-0-7660-3680-2
  1. Sharks—Juvenile literature. 2. Dolphins—Juvenile literature. I. Title.
  QL638.9.S845 2011
  597.3—dc22

                    2010003280

Paperback ISBN 978-1-59845-239-6
Printed in the United States of America
102010 Lake Book Manufacturing, Inc., Melrose Park, IL

10 9 8 7 6 5 4 3 2 1

To Our Readers: We have done our best to make sure all Internet Addresses in this book were active and appropriate when we went to press. However, the author and the publisher have no control over and assume no liability for the material available on those Internet sites or on other Web sites they may link to. Any comments or suggestions can be sent by e-mail to comments@enslow.com or to the address on the back cover.

♻ Enslow Publishers, Inc., is committed to printing our books on recycled paper. The paper in every book contains 10% to 30% post-consumer waste (PCW). The cover board on the outside of each book contains 100% PCW. Our goal is to do our part to help young people and the environment too!

Photo Credits: © iStockphoto.com: Chris Dascher pp. 4, 18, Debra McGuire, p. 15; © Minden Pictures: Hiroya Minakuchi, p. 17, Tui De Roy, p. 11; PacificStock/Photolibrary, p. 13; Photo Researchers, Inc.: Eye of Science, p. 8, Francois Gohier, p. 21, Michael Patrick O'Neill, p. 16; © SeaPics.com, pp. 14, 20; Shutterstock.com, pp. 1, 2, 5, 6, 7, 9, 10, 12, 19.

Cover Photos: © Mike Parry / Minden Pictures (left), Shutterstock.com (right).

Note to Parents and Teachers: The *Which Animal Is Which?* series supports the National Science Education Standards for K–4 science. The Words to Know section introduces subject-specific vocabulary words, including pronunciation and definitions. Early readers may need help with these new words.

Sayville Library
88 Greene Avenue
Sayville, NY 11782

JUL 2 1 2011

DISCARDED BY
SAYVILLE LIBRARY